Dinosaurs

by Annabelle Lynch

W

FRANKLIN WATTS

LONDON•SYDNEY

Franklin Watts

First published in Great Britain in 2015 by The Watts Publishing Group

Copyright © 2015 The Watts Publishing Group

Series editor: Julia Bird
Series consultant: Catherine Glavina
Series designer: Peter Scoulding

Picture acknowledgements: Linda Bucklin/Shutterstock: 1. Catmando/Shutterstock: 14-15. Computer Earth/Shutterstock: 18-19. Elenarts/Shutterstock: 10, 17, 22bl. iurii/Shutterstock: 4-5. Ozja/Shutterstock: 22cl. Prisma Archivo/Alamy: 6, 22cr. Jose Angel Astor Rocha/Shutterstock: 22tl. Michael Rosskothen/Shutterstock: front cover, 12-13. Marcio Silva/Alamy: 20-21, 22tr. Stocktrek Images Inc/Alamy: 8-9.

HB ISBN: 978 1 4451 3856 5
PB ISBN: 978 1 4451 3858 9

Dewey number: 560

Printed in China

Franklin Watts
An imprint of
Hachette Children's Group
Part of The Watts Publishing Group
Carmelite House
50 Victoria Embankment
London EC4Y 0DZ

An Hachette UK Company
www.hachette.co.uk

www.franklinwatts.co.uk

MIX
Paper from
responsible sources
FSC® C104740

FSC
www.fsc.org

Contents

What were dinosaurs?

Dinosaurs were animals
called reptiles. They
lived millions of
years ago.

Hatching
from eggs

Baby dinosaurs hatched from eggs. The eggs were laid in a nest.

Large
dinosaurs

The biggest dinosaur was Dreadnoughtus (dred-nor-tus).

It was heavier
than an
aeroplane!

Little
dinosaurs

The smallest dinosaur
was Compsognathus
(komp-sog-nay-thus).
It was about the same
size as a chicken.

Meat -eaters

Some dinosaurs ate other animals. Tyrannosaurus rex (tye-ran-a-sawr-us rex) was a fierce hunter.

Plant
-eaters

Some dinosaurs ate plants. Diplodocus (di-plod-uk-us) had a long neck to reach the top of trees.

Land
and sea

A Spinosaurus
(spy-nuh-saw-rus) was
a dinosaur that could
swim. It lived on land
and on sea.

Ready
to fight

Triceratops (try-sair-a-tops)
had three sharp horns.
The horns kept it safe.

Fossils

We find out about
dinosaurs from
fossils. Fossils show us
the shape a dinosaur
has left in rock.

Word bank

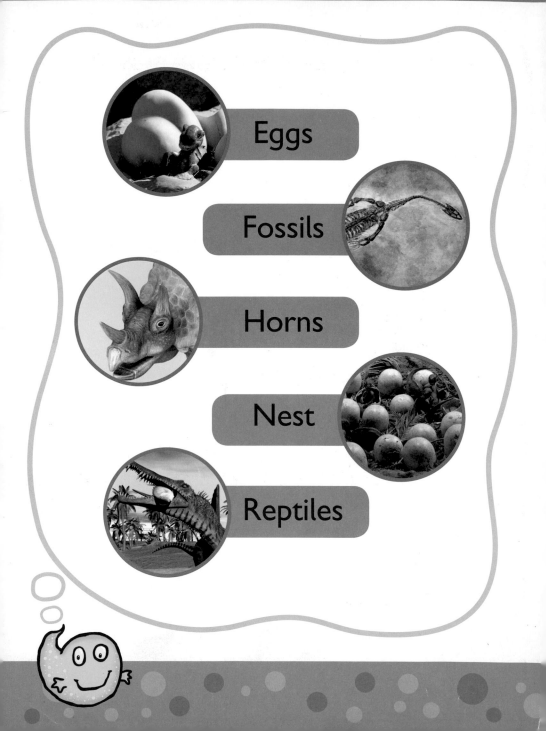

Eggs

Fossils

Horns

Nest

Reptiles

Quiz

1. Dinosaurs were animals called

a) rats
b) cats
c) reptiles.

2. The smallest dinosaur was the

a) Dreadnoughtus
b) Compsognathus
c) Spinosaurus.

3. Triceratops had three sharp

a) ears
b) feet
c) horns.

Turn over for answers!

Notes for adults

TADPOLES are structured to provide support for newly independent readers. The books may also be used by adults for sharing with young children.

Starting to read alone can be daunting. **TADPOLES** help by providing visual support and repeating words and phrases. These books will both develop confidence and encourage reading and rereading for pleasure.

If you are reading this book with a child, here are a few suggestions:

1. Make reading fun! Choose a time to read when you and the child are relaxed and have time to share the book.

2. Talk about the content of the book before you start reading. Look at the front cover and blurb. What expectations are raised about the content? Why might the child enjoy it? What connections can the child make with their own experience of the world?

3. If a word is phonically decodable, encourage the child to use a 'phonics first' approach to tackling new words by sounding the words out.

4. Invite the child to talk about the content after reading, returning to favourite pages and pictures. Extend vocabulary by examining the Word Bank and by discussing new concepts.

5. Give praise! Remember that small mistakes need not always be corrected.

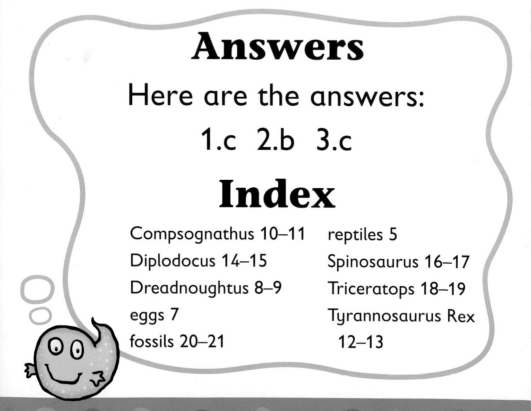

Answers

Here are the answers:

1.c 2.b 3.c

Index